The Horse and the Bell

Retold by Beverley Randell
From *The Bell of Atri*
Illustrated by Margaret Power

Once upon a time, many years ago,
a good king ruled over a town in Italy.

He would not allow
anyone in his kingdom
to be cruel or unfair to anyone else.

In the middle of the town,
beside the market place,
there was a tall tower with a bell.

"If people need my help
because a cruel thing
has been done to them," said the king,
"they must ring the bell.
Then I will come to the tower
and listen to what they have to say."

For many years,
no one in the kingdom rang the bell.

Every child was cared for.
Sick people were cared for.

No one was cruel, or unfair, or unkind.

Then, one day,
a soldier looked at his old horse.
"You are too old
to carry me around any more," he said.
"Why should I go on feeding you?"

He struck the horse with his hand,
and sent him away down the dusty road.

At first the old horse wandered about,
feeding from the bushes and grass
by the roadside.

But soon the weather grew colder.
It was wintertime,
and snow covered the ground.

Now the poor old horse
could find very little to eat.
He walked with a limp
and his mane grew ragged.
He grew thinner and thinner
as the weeks went by.

When the winter ended at last,
the people in the kingdom were glad.
They tied spring flowers and leaves
to their doorways.
They put tables out in the sunshine
in the market place.
They spread the tables with plates of food.
Then they sat down with their king
to have a feast to welcome the spring.

No one saw the starving horse
limp up to the bell tower
and go underneath the arch.
He began to eat the leaves
that were tied to the bell rope.
He tugged at the leaves with his teeth,
and this made the rope move.

Ding-dong! Ding-dong! Ding-dong!
rang the bell in the high tower.

Everyone gasped,
and the king rose to his feet.
"Who is ringing the bell?" he asked.
"What cruel thing has been done?"

The king led the way to the tower.
There he found the old horse,
with the bell rope in his mouth.
The king was shocked
when he saw how thin and miserable
the horse was.

"This horse is nothing but skin and bone,"
he said. "Who owns him?"

The king looked at the people
standing near him.
"Does anyone know who owns
this poor animal?" he asked again.

The soldier was afraid.
He looked down at the ground.

"I think this horse belongs to you,"
said the king sternly,
looking at the soldier.
"Why is he so thin? Answer me!"

"I sent my horse away because he was old,"
said the soldier. "He was no use to me.
I thought he would find
enough to eat by the roadside.
I did not mean to be cruel."

Everyone waited
to hear what the king had to say.

"I am always angry when I see that animals
have been badly treated," said the king.
"Perhaps we should send **you** away
from the kingdom!"

The soldier fell to his knees
in front of the king and said,
"Now I see that
it was a cruel thing to do,
and I am very sorry."

"Well," said the king to the soldier,
"because you are sorry,
I will give you a second chance.
I will not make you leave the kingdom
after all.
But from now on you must
take good care of your horse.
You must feed him well
and be kind to him.
You must show us
that you have mended your ways."

So the soldier took his horse home.
There he gave him food to eat,
water to drink,
and a warm stable to live in
for the rest of his days.